DRUGS AND DRIVING

Drug use is one of the most common causes of serious traffic accidents.

DRUGS AND DRIVING

Janet Grosshandler

THE ROSEN PUBLISHING GROUP, INC.
NEW YORK

The people pictured in this book are only models; they, in no way, practice or endorse the activities illustrated. Captions serve only to explain the subjects of photographs and do not in any way imply a connection between the real-life models and the staged situations.

Published in 1992 by The Rosen Publishing Group, Inc.
29 East 21st Street, New York, NY 10010

First Edition

Printed in the United States of America.

Library of Congress Cataloging-in-Publication Data

Grosshandler, Janet.
    Drugs and driving / Janet Grosshandler.
    (The Drug Abuse Prevention Library)
    Includes bibliographical references and index.
    Summary: Discusses the use of drugs by teenagers, and, in particular, the consequences of combining drugs and driving.
        ISBN 0-8239-1417-8
        1. Automobile drivers—United States—Drug use—Juvenile literature. [1. Automobile drivers—Drug use. 2. Drug abuse. 3. Drinking and traffic accidents. 4. Traffic accidents.] I. Title.
    II. Series.
    HE5620.D65G76 1992
    363.1'251—dc20   92-6146
                                     CIP
                                     AC

Contents

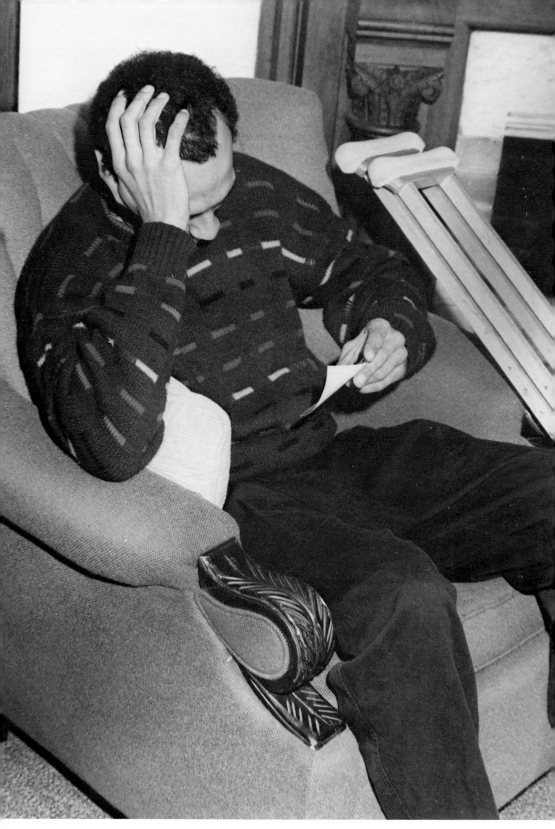

Being responsible for the death of a friend is a heavy burden.

CHAPTER 1

A.J.'s Story

"It was just a regular weekend party," said A.J., 17. "We did this all the time."

"This" was hitting the local party scene. Scoring some grass, tapping the keg, hanging out at the mall, and then cruising the neighborhoods was the Friday routine for A.J. and his friends. Pete, Robert, and Leon never thought that this Friday night would be any different. Neither did A.J.

"I got a little wasted, so I let Pete drive my dad's car," A.J. said. "Pete didn't have much beer. We thought he'd be okay."

Pete thought he was okay, too. He stumbled as he got into the driver's seat.

8

"Everything was cool. Then something weird happened," A.J. said. "Pete wanted to race the car on the beltway."

A.J., sitting in the front passenger seat, slammed his foot on an imaginary brake as Pete crossed over and crashed into the highway divider. The car jolted back into the lane. It was hit from behind by a minivan driven by a young woman and her four-year-old daughter.

The impact sent the boys off the road into a telephone pole.

"In my nightmares I still hear the metal crash as we hit the pole," A.J. said. "Then I felt this terrible pain in my legs. I was wedged in and couldn't move."

A.J. took a deep breath before he could go on. "They found Robert about 10 feet away down in the ditch. He was dead. I was still alive, but I remember wishing I would die, I hurt so bad.

"From where I was I could see Pete. That stupid jerk didn't even have his seat belt on. He had crashed through the windshield. I wanted to call to him but nothing came out.

"I thought for a second how mad my father was going to be because we wrecked his car. That's when I realized that Pete was dead. He wasn't moving or anything. I closed my eyes and just prayed that someone would come and help us."

A.J. was the only one who survived the crash. It took almost two hours to pry him out of the wreck.

The young woman and her daughter also went off the road, smashing through the guardrail and flipping over twice. They were wearing their seat belts, but the impact was too much. They both died.

"We didn't think something like this could ever happen," A.J. said. "I thought I was doing the right thing because I didn't drive when I was high. I was even wearing my seat belt. But Pete and Robert weren't. Maybe if they had been, they would still be alive. Maybe that lady and her little girl would still be here. Maybe . . . maybe . . . maybe . . . ."

A.J. will live with what happened for the rest of his life.

"I guess I learned my lesson the hard way. When kids ask me to party, I always remember Pete and Robert. I try to tell my other friends not to get near a car if they're high. The worst for me is that I can't get that lady and her little girl out of my mind. We wiped out their lives in two seconds. That's something I'll have to live with forever."

Hundreds of thousands of people are killed or injured in drug-related car accidents each year.

CHAPTER 2

Overview

*A*merican teenagers are killing others and themselves at an alarming rate in car crashes. Drugged drivers kill themselves and thousands of innocent people by getting behind the wheel when they are high.

Each year in these accidents, hundreds of thousands of people are maimed, scarred, paralyzed, and burned . The numbers average out to about one person every minute of every day. When you get in a car, your chances of being in an accident are one in seven. When you get in a car a little bit high or with a drugged driver, your chances rise to one in three. Are those the kinds of odds you want to bet your life on?

12   Alcohol is the drug that gets the most publicity because it is the drug that teens use most often. However, it is not the only drug that can affect your ability to drive. Using marijuana, cocaine, crack, amphetamines, and barbiturates makes you a menace on the highway. Drugs blur your vision and affect your reflexes, coordination, and judgment.

    Some over-the-counter medicines that you can buy in a drugstore can affect your driving ability, too. Sleeping pills, cough medicines, allergy pills, and cold remedies may contain amphetamines (called "speed" on the street), which can interfere with your driving. Read the labels on medicine bottles you might have at home. A lot of them contain alcohol and carry warnings not to drive or operate machinery when using them. These medicines may also cause drowsiness, sleeplessness, nervousness, and irritability. If you are taking one of them, you are "driving under the influence." And if you combine it with a few beers, you can be arrested for DUI.

    Any drug, including alcohol, can mess up your ability to make safe judgments and interfere with your vision and driving ability. All your driving skills are dulled.

Eighty percent (eight out of ten) of fatal accidents are first accidents. To say, "I've never had a single accident," is no excuse to take driving lightly. The statistics show that teenagers are at huge risk for accidents because they don't have years of experience with driving. They certainly can't handle driving while high on drugs. Too many teens and young adults kill themselves and others because they mix drugs and driving.

In addition to the terrible sadness brought to families when one member is involved in a car crash, the financial costs of drugged driving are staggering. Medical expenses, property damage, court costs, lawyers' fees, and time lost from school or work can soar to hundreds of thousands of dollars for *each* accident.

If you are arrested and convicted of drugged driving, you face time in jail, fines of hundreds or thousands of dollars, community service, loss of your driver's license, and possibly cancellation of insurance. If you cause a death or serious injuries in an accident or are involved in more than one accident, you could be charged with a felony. That means you face a prison sentence on conviction.

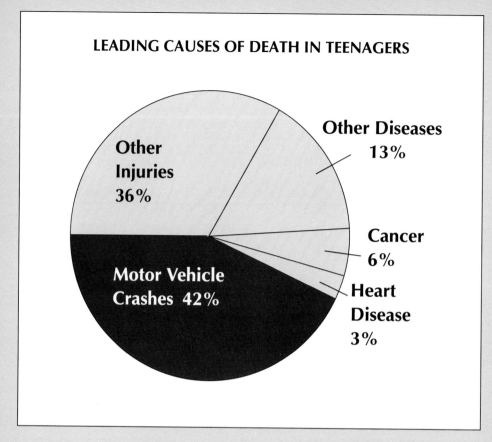

LEADING CAUSES OF DEATH IN TEENAGERS

Other Injuries 36%

Other Diseases 13%

Cancer 6%

Heart Disease 3%

Motor Vehicle Crashes 42%

FACT: In America, over one million people suffer crippling and other serious injuries every year because of drunk and drugged drivers.

FACT: Every driver has a 50 percent chance of being in an accident related to drugged driving in his or her lifetime.

FACT: Young people (ages 16 to 24) cause 44 percent of drunk and drugged driving accidents. The same age group makes up only 22 percent of all drivers.

FACT: One American life is lost *every 23 minutes* in a drunk or drugged driving accident.

More teenagers are dying from car accidents than from anything else. One of the major contributors to these accidents is the use of drugs, including alcohol.

Driving is one of the first big steps you take toward becoming an adult. Getting your license means freedom—and new independence.

Alcohol and other drugs can give you a false sense of control. You're cruising along, driving fast, with the radio turned up loud. You're feeling high and pretty loose. Watch out for that curve! You're going too fast! The side of your car that gets wrapped around the tree is where your best friend is sitting. The car you're driving has turned into a lethal weapon.

"What can I do about it? I'm only one kid," you say. "I can't make any difference."

Yes, you can. If once, just once, you stop someone from driving under the influence of drugs, you may very well have saved a life. If you put away your keys and refuse to get behind the steering wheel when you are high, you may well save your own life. You can make a difference if you make safe decisions about drugs and driving.

CHAPTER 3

What Drugs Do to You

*A*nything you put into your body has an effect. If you eat nutritious fruits and vegetables, your body will be healthier. If you feed yourself lots of sugar and junk food, your body will be affected in a nonhealthy way.

Drinking, eating, smoking, or in any way absorbing drugs into your body will cause things to happen. You learn about drugs in school, on TV, from your family and friends. Some teens still don't want to believe that doing any kind of drug, no matter how little or how seldom, will hurt them. Read this information and use it to make safe, healthy decisions for yourself about using drugs.

Everything you put into your body affects you. Taking care of yourself means eating nutritious foods that help you feel good.

18   *Tobacco smoke* is inhaled into your body. Where there is smoke, there is always a danger to your health. The smoke follows a path in your body starting in your mouth, moving through your throat and into your windpipe. Then it travels through your bronchial tubes and finally into your lungs.

This smoke that you inhale is made up of nicotine, gases, and tars. The gases include carbon dioxide, carbon monoxide (poisonous), ammonia (irritates body tissues), and others. Organic compounds in the smoke include alcohols (minor irritants), phenols (cancer-producing substances), and others that cause cancer and are poisonous.

A drug called *nicotine* is also in tobacco smoke. Nicotine affects your nerves and muscles, the pupils of your eyes, your taste buds, and your blood pressure. It also speeds up your heartbeat. It touches and affects just about every system in your body. The tars from the smoke coat your bronchial tubes and lungs. They clog your lungs and make you cough. The nicotine and tars in the smoke interfere with how body cells form in your lungs. That is how lung cancer starts.

The main killers of "heavy" smokers are coronary heart disease, lung cancer, and emphysema.

Alcohol, another commonly used drug, goes directly into your bloodstream and is sent to all parts and systems of your body. Your reflexes, coordination, memory, and judgment undergo changes. You may stagger, have slurred speech and double vision, experience mood changes, and even become unconscious.

If you drink a large amount, you could die, because alcohol depresses the part of your brain that controls your breathing and heart rate.

Hallucinogens are drugs that change your ability to sense and perceive what is real and unreal. The illusion that you experience may range from feeling "high" or euphoric (like being detached or free-floating) all the way to seeing, hearing, and sensing things that are not really there.

Marijuana (also called "pot," "grass," "reefer," "smoke," "weed," "shake") contains a compound called *THC*. The THC is absorbed into your lungs, brain, and liver. It can stay in your body for days and can cause a great deal of damage.

Alcohol and nicotine are addictive substances that can also pose a risk to health.

Smoking marijuana can damage your lungs and impair the brain functions of thinking, learning, and remembering. It can make you feel insecure or frightened, uninterested and uncaring, or even paranoid (suspicious and afraid). Even though pot used to be thought of as a "harmless" weed, all research points to the fact that it is a dangerous drug. For many kids, it is the first "illegal" drug they try after using the "legal" drugs tobacco and alcohol.

Another hallucinogen is *phencyclidine,* known as "PCP" or "angel dust." In small doses, PCP has effects like those of alcohol: poor coordination, slurred speech, mental confusion, sleepiness, and numbness in fingers and toes. Users may also tend to feel nauseated and may vomit.

In large doses, PCP can act like an anesthetic, a drug used to put you to sleep before an operation. Your senses may be disturbed or blocked. You may feel left out, alone, and isolated. In some people, these effects have lasted up to ten days.

PCP can also cause terrible depression, severe mental suffering, or *flashbacks*. People have died from PCP.

Another hallucinogen that causes mind changes is "LSD" or "acid." Even in tiny doses, LSD causes the pupils of your eyes to dilate, your blood pressure to rise, your heart to beat irregularly, and the muscles of your internal organs to contract. The effects begin slowly and mildly, then in a while the hallucinations start. You "see" sounds or "hear" colors more intensely.

An acid "trip" jumbles real and unreal images and feelings. It can quickly turn into a horror show, and the user can be driven into a state of violent insanity. The effects of LSD can last for hours. Later, inactive parts of the drug that remain in your body may become active again, and you may have another LSD trip against your will. That is a flashback, and it may haunt you for a long time.

PCP and LSD are drugs of terror. Your mind is altered with their use, in some cases even permanently.

Drugs that speed up the activities of the cells in the central nervous system are called *stimulants*. Caffeine in your coffee, tea, and cola and the nicotine in your cigarettes are examples of stimulants that occur naturally in plants.

Other stimulants are human-made. They are called *amphetamines* and are used to treat certain illnesses. They have been declared illegal in many states.

Amphetamines are usually made in the form of capsules, tablets, or powder. Some people mix amphetamines with heroin in trying to get a longer high. This can sometimes be fatal.

Amphetamines affect your body by speeding up your heart rate and other body functions . You feel excitable, and your speech is fast and unclear. You are restless, and your hands shake. You may perspire and experience sleeplessness.

Other effects include nervousness, fears, memory lapses, irritability, or hallucinations. Headaches, dizziness, blurred vision, and heart irregularities are also possible. Using amphetamines can lead to dependency.

Even though alcohol is a legal drug, responsible teenagers know
its dangers and turn it down.

24 The drug *cocaine* is sometimes called a *superstimulant*, even though it is classified as a *narcotic*. Cocaine is used by snorting or injecting it. It acts immediately on the central nervous system. Your pulse rate and respiration increase. Your body temperature rises, and so does your blood pressure. When the drug reaches your bloodstream you feel a "rush," a high that may last half an hour.

People have different reactions to cocaine. Some feel energetic, others say they can think more clearly. These reactions are short-lived. Many users experience depression when the effects of cocaine wear off. Heavy users often become more aggressive and anxious. Mood swings and memory losses have also been reported. Habitual "coke" users may experience convulsions or even become paralyzed.

Crack is the street name given to freebased (purified and concentrated) co-caine. It looks like shavings or slivers of soap. Crack is sold in small bottles, in folding papers, or in heavy tinfoil. It is usually smoked in a pipe. Crack addicts become obsessed by the drug.

Solvents are volatile substances that people sniff or inhale. Glue, airplane glue,

lighter fluid, nail-polish remover, cleaning
fluids, and gasoline are commonly abused.
Solvents are mainly abused by children
ranging in age from 8 to 16.

25

Some of the signs and symptoms of
glue sniffing are a runny nose, chemical
odor on the breath and clothes, double
vision, foul breath, watering eyes,
staggering walk, slurred speech, and
drowsiness. Periodic violent acts against
themselves are also traits of glue sniffers.

Safe driving requires a clear head and sound judgment.

Drugs can affect coordination and make simple tasks impossible.

Young people who sniff glue may turn to using other dangerous household chemicals in search of a high. Important organs of your body can be destroyed if you regularly inhale such solvents. The fumes can seriously hurt you.

Narcotics are drugs that bring about sleep or sluggishness and at the same time relieve pain. Painkilling drugs usually come from *opium*. You may be familiar with codeine or morphine, which are used in hospitals or when you are sick. All narcotics that come from opium or are human-made, like Demerol, are capable of addicting the user. That means that your body always craves more of the drug.

Opiates slow down your respiratory system. Your oxygen intake can be so much reduced that you stop breathing and die.

Heroin is an opiate. It is not much of a painkiller, but it is highly addictive. Needle marks, infections, the spread of AIDS by use of dirty needles, and blood diseases are part of a heroin junkie's life.

Getting involved with narcotics is a losing game. Your body tissues build up a tolerance, and you need to use more drugs to feed your craving for the high.

28   *Sedatives* are other drugs that affect the central nervous system. But instead of speeding it up like stimulants, sedatives depress or slow body activities such as breathing, blood pressure, heartbeat, and cell function.

Barbiturates are sedatives that are used to treat some medical problem or to make people sleep. They are often used to relax some patients before and during surgery. Unfortunately, these drugs seem to be overprescribed because they tranquilize the user. They can become habit-forming.

If you take barbiturates, your reactions and responses are slowed, your speech is slurred and mixed up, and you feel slug-gish. Your thinking becomes muddled, and your behavior may be up and down. An overdose can cause death.

All of the above descriptions are brief. But make no mistake, books can be written about each drug and its dangers. If you become involved with any of these drugs, you take risks with all aspects of your life—your health, your mental stability, your family, your relationships, your present and your future, for as long as you *have* a future.

CHAPTER 4

High School Habits

*T*hink about the following statistics:

- One out of 10 people who drink becomes an alcoholic. There are about 17 million alcoholics in America, 4.5 million of whom are teenagers.
- One out of 20 high-school seniors drinks alcohol daily.
- The average age for first smoking cigarettes is 11; for drinking alcohol, 12; and for smoking marijuana, 13.
- In 1987, three out of eight high-school seniors said that, in the past two weeks, they had five drinks or more in a row at least once.
- Teenagers are the only age group in which the death rate has *increased* in the

30 past 20 years, largely due to drinking/driving accidents.

• Fifty-seven percent of high-school seniors have tried an illegal drug, and 36 percent have tried drugs other than marijuana.

• Over 6 percent of sixth to eighth graders (11- to 14-year-olds) have smoked marijuana, and about 2 percent smoke it at least weekly.

• In 1987, in a survey of thousands of seniors, 5.6 percent reported having tried crack, and 4 percent said they had used it in the past year.

• Daily smoking of cigarettes has not declined among high-school seniors since 1984.

• The average time for an adult to become an alcoholic is 10 to 15 years. The average time for a teenager to become one is 10 to 15 *months*. The average time for a preteen is 10 to 15 weeks.

Going with the Crowd

"I can sit in homeroom on a Monday morning," said Jemal, 17, "and hear about who drank what and who snorted what at all the weekend parties. It's like no one really tries to keep it a secret anymore."

Many "legal" over-the-counter drugs can affect driving ability.
Always read warning labels.

Letting a friend drive if you have had alcohol is the responsible thing to do.

"In my crowd," said Les, 16, "probably **33** 80 to 90 percent drink a couple of weekends a month. There's not much else to do, I guess. Last week some kids were doing acid, but not everyone wanted to try it."

Depending on your crowd, your friends may not drink, may drink a little, or they may push drinking as a requirement to stay in the crowd. The decisions you make about whether to put drugs/alcohol in your body can affect many aspects of your life—acceptance by your peers, dealings with your parents, sexual relationships, schoolwork, run-ins with police, and more.

Most teenage passenger deaths happen when another teen has been driving. Some 42 percent of motor vehicle deaths of 13- to 17-year-old passengers in 1987 happened when they got in a car with a 16- or 17-year-old behind the wheel.

Per-mile facts for 1987 show that teenagers are involved in twice the number of alcohol-related fatal crashes as are drivers in the 30- to 40-year age group. That's a sobering fact when you consider that there are probably more older drivers on the road than there are teenagers. Does that make teenagers less responsible? Does it make them more reckless and daring?

34   A survey of high-school seniors reported that the percentage of drivers having one or more moving violations (running a stop sign or a red light, speeding, etc.) in a 12-month period went up by almost 7 percent from 1982 to 1987. Almost 5 percent reported having been ticketed for a moving violation after using alcohol in the same 12 months. In total, the survey indicated that more than 36 percent of those high-school seniors who were ticketed or arrested for moving violations were driving under the influence.

"My friends and I were stopped a few weeks ago," said José, 16. "The cop asked if we had been drinking and we said no. Then he gave Brad a speeding ticket and let us go. And we were pretty drunk. So maybe there's even more of that going on."

Statistics are not always 100 percent right. But if the above information is 80 or 90 percent correct, it still is too many kids getting high, drunk, hurt, and killed on the road.

CHAPTER 5

How Drugs Interfere with Your Driving Skills

*C*onsider this. You are riding in your older sister's car. As you cruise down a busy street, the radio is blasting and you are enjoying yourself. All of a sudden a van comes out of the cross street right in front of you. "Look out!" you yell. Your sister slams on the brakes, checks quickly in the rearview mirror, and swerves to the right, narrowly missing the "idiot" who ran the stop sign. Hearts pounding, you look at each other and breathe a sigh of relief. You're safe.

Now consider this. You are riding in your older sister's car. As you cruise down the same busy street, your sister is lighting

36 up her third cigarette. She had a couple of beers just before she picked you up, and she's giggling at a joke the DJ on the radio just told that wasn't very funny to you.

All of a sudden a van comes out of the cross street right in front of you. "Look out!" you yell. Your sister drops her cigarette, burning her arm, and slams on the brakes. She forgets to check the rear-view mirror and pulls to the right, forcing the car behind you off the road into the guardrail. She has only one hand on the wheel, so she doesn't pull far enough to the right and smashes into the rear end of the van that ran the stop sign.

Pretty different endings, right? As much as teenagers want to think that they are "fine" to drive after using drugs, it is a proven fact that drugs interfere with the skills you need to be a safe driver.

Reaction time is how quickly you respond to something that happens. Slamming on your brakes, pulling to the right to avoid hitting the car in front of you, honking your horn—all take a split second to do. Common drugs like alcohol and barbiturates depress your ability to function. You can't react in the split second it takes to avoid an accident.

A good driver must be able to react quickly to unexpected situations.

38

Eye focus is important when you drive. Stop signs, traffic signs, and people on the side of the road will appear as you drive. Seeing everything clearly is a requirement. You have to pass a vision test to get your license. When you drive after doing drugs you can't focus or see clearly.

Peripheral vision is the ability to see things that are not right in front of you. Billboards, houses, other cars, and street signs pass on both sides when you are cruising down the street. You need to be able to see when a car pulls out of a driveway or intersection, or when the car next to you pulls up to change lanes.

A study was done to test how alcohol affects peripheral vision. A person with a blood-alcohol content (BAC) of .55 (that's only one or two drinks in two hours for some people) loses almost one third of peripheral vision on a field-of-vision test.

Your speed also affects peripheral vision. The faster you go, the less you are able to see things on the side. People sometimes feel "up" from a drug, have a false sense of confidence, and are not afraid to drive fast. When you speed while feeling the effects of a drug, you'll see very little except a blurry, distorted scene right in front of you.

Time-sharing skill is the ability to pay attention to doing several things at the same time. The computer in your brain observes all that is out there in front of you. It decides what you need to do to get where you want to go.

Beginning drivers have not had the years of experience it takes to put together all the information you get as you drive. All your attention and skills are needed to be a safe driver, and even the best drivers may be involved in accidents that are no fault of theirs. If you add the effects of drugs, loud music pouring out of the tape deck, and the noise from other kids in the car, you cut down on the time-sharing skills you need to drive safely and increase the odds of having an accident.

Night vision is something that cats are known for. We have a harder time seeing in the dark. When you drive at night, your vision can be reduced by as much as half. Drugging yourself, especially with alcohol, reduces the oxygen in your bloodstream, which affects your vision. Then you drive with even less night vision than when you are sober and straight.

Any drug is a mind-altering substance. When you combine drugs, the effects are increased. Certain drugs may make you

Night driving takes extra concentration because vision is greatly reduced.

feel stimulated. You feel flushed. Small amounts of alcohol can do that. Your heart beats faster, and you lose some of your inhibitions. You feel freer to talk, laugh, and fool around. Then you climb into the driver's seat.

"When I drink I feel like I'm on top of the world at first," Kenny said. "Last Friday night my friends and I played a mean game of 'chicken'—you know, when you keep passing each other? I'm not so scared when I feel high."

When you are drugging and drinking, taking risks seems less frightening. Your emotions and brain undergo changes when you put drugs in your body. Kids take risks they never would take if they were straight.

"I'm all right to drive" is often heard after a party. Believing that your driving skills remain good when you are drinking and drugging is common. In one study, drivers knocked over orange cones and ran down flags, but they still thought they drove as well as when they were sober. To be a safe driver and reduce your chances of accidents, you need to be alert, sharp, and in control. Drugs interfere with your brain, your emotions, your coordination, and every skill you need to drive.

CHAPTER 6

The Law

Famous last words:
"I'm a better driver when I drink."
"I've gotten home safely often enough."
"He's okay to drive."

Some teens use these statements as if to prove that they'll never have an accident. Okay, so you made it home this time. What about the next time? Or the next, when your boyfriend chugs a six-pack and then gets behind the wheel? Driving after drinking is a big gamble.

DUI (Driving Under the Influence) or DWI (Driving While Intoxicated) is one of the biggest gambles you can take with your life. It is hard to tell how much of a drug a person can take and still drive

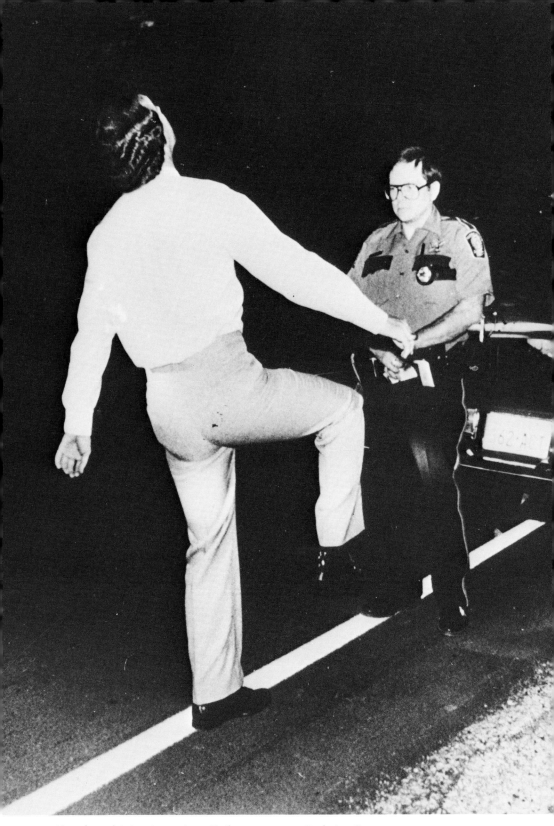

Drunken driving is a crime. Failure to pass a "sobriety" test may lead to arrest.

44 safely. It differs with each person. How much alcohol you have in your blood or how much pot you've smoked is what determines your condition.

Suspicion and Arrest!

If you or your friends are pulled over because you are suspected of DUI, you'll be asked to do some things to determine your blood-alcohol content. You will be asked to take a test to measure how alert and coordinated you are.

Walking a straight line, touching your nose, and reciting tongue twisters will help decide if you are not sober. You can also blow into a breath tester, which measures the percentage of alcohol in your body. If you refuse these tests, your license can be suspended for 30 days.

You *have* to take the test to prove you are innocent. It may seem like losing your freedom, but crashing into someone, hurting or possibly killing another person, takes away his or her freedom. When you get your license you agree to be tested any time for BAC. This agreement is called *implied consent*.

If your breath measures .10 or higher, it means that you are legally drunk or *intoxicated*. In some states a reading between .05 and .10 means that you are legally *impaired*. You may be taken to a hospital for urine and blood tests.

If your blood-alcohol content is .10 or higher, you will be arrested for DUI. Some state laws now permit arrest for a BAC between .05 and .10.

Being arrested is a serious matter—and it can be expensive. You have to pay the lawyer's fees and fines. You could also possibly spend time in jail.

Conviction

Your court date arrives. All the results of the breath test, urine test, and blood test are presented. The judge studies the evidence and pronounces your sentence.

Sentence? But I'm not a criminal!

Yes, you are. DUI is a criminal activity with consequences if you're convicted.

Fines. The laws differ in each state, but you will pay fines of from $250 to $1,000 if you are convicted.

Jail. You may have to stay in jail from 48 hours up to a year. Some states permit community service, for example, helping others, instead of jail.

Rehabilitation. A driver improvement program is usually required if you are found guilty of DUI. Many states make

46   you go through a local alcohol or drug rehabilitation program in order to help you straighten out your drug problem.

Probation. Instead of jail time, some states put you on probation for anywhere from one to three years. A probation officer checks with your family, school, and job to make sure you are staying straight and sober. And you have to report to your probation officer at specific times.

License revocation. Remember those weeks and months of waiting until you finally got your license? Remember all the practice you had to do? Being licensed to drive seemed like the real beginning of adult freedom. But it also represents adult responsibility.

If you are convicted of DUI, you lose your license for at least a few months and possibly as long as a year. You give up the freedom because you abused the personal responsibility.

Money problems. How much do you think it costs to fight a DUI arrest and court procedure? Add to that the fines you'll have to pay, and you'll discover that your savings account won't even begin to cover the costs.

Family problems. Being found guilty of DUI will take its toll on your family, too.

Arguments, accusations, denials, and breakups can happen. Your name may be published in the newspaper.

Job loss. No wheels, no job. If your employer can't rely on you to get to work, you may lose your job. There goes your paycheck, causing more money problems. Getting a new job may be hard, too. Some job applications ask if you've ever been convicted of a crime. DUI is a crime.

Many states adopt newer and stricter drug laws every year. These laws tie in with your driver's license. If you are found guilty of a drug offense, you will lose your license from six months up to two years.

Each state has its own laws against drunk and drugged driving. Check with your police department or the state motor vehicle bureau for the law in your state. Your driver's education teacher also has the information. It is important to know what you risk when you get behind that wheel while drugged.

The good news is that the numbers of accidents and deaths from DUI have fallen in the past 10 years. That's because the number of arrests and convictions has gone up. Don't become part of the sorry statistics. The only way to drive is sober and straight.

In an accident situation, fractions of a second in reaction time can mean the difference between life and death.

CHAPTER 7

The Aftermath of Drugs and Driving

"**I** turned 18 just a week before the accident," Todd said. "It was a regular summer party, no big drinking going on. I had a couple of beers and smoked a little grass. But I wasn't staggering or slurring my words. I felt fine."

When Todd left the party he made a wide left-hand turn. Passing too close to the sidewalk, he tried to swing his car back into the lane. As he looked back, he saw no police cars and sighed with relief.

As Todd turned his attention back to the road in front of him, he didn't have time to avoid his second driving mistake of the night.

50

"It happened so fast. I guess I was too high to think clearly, because I couldn't swerve out of the way in time," he said.

A 15-year-old girl had started to cross the street but began to retreat to the curb when she saw Todd's car coming. In a 25 mph area, he was doing 40. She didn't reach the safety of the sidewalk in time. Todd's car struck her.

At the police station, Todd's blood-alcohol content registered .12 on the Intoxilizer test. He was arrested and spent the night in jail.

The next day, he found out that the girl had died and that he was being charged with manslaughter by auto.

"When I think back to that night, I know that I could have made different decisions. When someone shoved a can of beer in my hand, I could have refused it. I didn't have to take a couple hits of grass. But they offered, and I did it. I knew it was wrong to get in the car to drive. I never thought this could happen to me."

Todd will live forever with the tragic consequences of his decisions that night. He was fined $25,000 and sentenced to probation for 10 years and 300 hours in schools as a spokesperson against drugs and driving.

• Laurie was a passenger in a car driven by her friend. A daytime wine party ended in a crash into a telephone pole. Laurie's leg was crushed. Gone was her college scholarship for track.

• Jess is paralyzed from the waist down, the result of an almost lethal combination of cocaine and his motorcycle. "I didn't think I was too high to drive. I felt like I was smooth."

• Randi was a straight-A student and president of her senior class. A 17-year-old driver changed her life forever. Injuries from the car accident left Randi a crippled paraplegic with contracted and spastic hands and feet. She will never leave her wheelchair. Randi was the innocent victim of another person's bad decisions.

Head injuries are common in accidents when drivers and passengers are not using seat belts. Statistics put together by Patrick O'Malley, Ph.D., and Lloyd Johnston, Ph.D., at the Institute for Social Research, University of Michigan, show how today's teens feel about using seatbelts. The researchers gave testimony at hearings before the National Commission Against Drunk Driving and the National Highway Traffic Safety Administration at Forth Worth, Texas, in March 1988.

52   The doctors reported the results of a survey of 17,000 seniors in their *Monitoring the Future* project.

PERCENTAGE OF SENIORS USING SEAT BELTS WHEN DRIVING

	1986	1987
Never, Seldom	43.2	36.7
Always	25.0	33.0

PERCENTAGE OF SENIORS USING SEAT BELTS AS PASSENGER IN FRONT SEAT

	1986	1987
Never, Seldom	46.6	39.0
Always	22.0	30.1

When you get into a car to drive while you are high or as a passenger with someone who is drugged by alcohol or other substances, you risk the following if you do not buckle up:

1. Cracking your head on the frame of the car, causing brain injuries.

2. Hitting your head and face into the windshield.

3. Shattering the windshield as your head and face smash through the shards of glass.

CHAPTER 8

What You Can Do

"My brother and his girlfriend had an accident coming home from a party," said Danielle, 15. "Tod was high and ran a stop sign. They crashed into another car. His girlfriend was thrown from the car and died. I've seen what he's going through. I don't want something like that to happen to me."

Danielle, with the help of a teacher at her school, started a **SAFE** program. SAFE stands for Substance Abuse Free Environment. The kids run promotions about staying straight, sober, and safe in situations where alcohol and other drugs threaten their well-being. Here are some other things you can do to protect the lives of the people in your community.

54 | ## *Project Graduation*

Project Graduation is a national alcohol and safety program designed to keep kids safe, healthy, and alive during prom and graduation time.

Participants try to:
- Have kids sign pledges not to drink or drug and drive.
- Set up a Safe Ride system.
- Promote a "Buckle-Up Day."

SADD

Students Against Drunk Driving are groups of high-school students who want to do something about the deadly combination of drinking and driving.

In 1981, Robert Anatas, Director of Health Education in the Wayland Public Schools in Massachusetts, organized the program in his schools. The idea spread quickly. To get information on how to start, write to Students Against Drunk Driving, P.O. Box 800, Marlboro, MA 01752.

Safe Rides for Teens

"Our high-school SADD group started a new idea this year," Mary Beth said. "We organized and operated a Safe Rides for Teens program to give kids rides home.

"Parent taxis" provide volunteer adults to drive teens to and from parties or proms.

"We cover the phone lines for our hotline number, and a volunteer parent or teacher and a student are on call on weekends to pick up kids."

Safe Rides takes much responsibility. You might ask a service organization in your town to work with you on the project.

Parent Taxis

Set up parent agreements with a few families that you know. Most families will work out this kind of arrangement if you ask and set up guidelines in advance.

Rent-a-Limo

When figuring out expenses for the junior and senior prom, many families add in the cost of renting a limousine for the evening.

"Our parents didn't want to worry about who was driving or what shape we were in," said Brett, 18. "So four couples and our parents chipped in and rented a limo for the prom. It was pretty cool!"

Radio and Media Announcements

When teens want to pitch a responsible message, radio and TV stations are usually agreeable to giving them air time. Media announcements for staying straight are likely to make it on the air.

Contests

Take your message down to the middle
and elementary schools by running slogan
and poster contests. Ask local businesses
and restaurants to donate prizes for the
younger kids to make a commitment to
staying straight, sober, and safe.

Be sure you are organized before you
try to sell this idea to your school. Giving
a responsible presentation will get you
respect and the approval to go ahead.

Organize a Rally

Put on a big assembly with speakers who
have had drunk driving tragedies or school-
mates who have lost a friend or relative to
drugs and driving. Plan for the police or
safety commission to do a car-crash dem-
onstration. Have a persuasive speaker get
the kids to take a pledge to stand up for
their own lives and the right to be safe
when they drive.

Peer Counseling

Peer counseling means kids helping kids.
It uses students as role models, helpers,
and leaders. Pairing up older, responsible
teens with younger ones who need help,
information, a contact, or a good influence
is usually successful.

Obeying important safety rules is part of being a responsible driver.

Do you sometimes feel that you have no power, that you can't change the world?

"I'm only one kid. What can I do?"

There's lots you can do right in your own little corner of the world. Working on a SADD organization, helping kids get safe rides, and being a role model can all make a difference.

It can save a life, including your own.

Glossary
Explaining New Words

alcoholic   Of or containing alcohol; a person suffering from alcoholism.

anesthetic   Drug used in medicine to numb the sense of feeling.

barbiturate   Any of various drugs used in medicine to make one sleep.

consequence   Result or outcome.

emphysema   Disease of the lungs that makes it difficult to breathe.

euphoric   Feeling relaxed, happy.

fatal   Causing death.

felony   A serious crime.

flashback   Hallucination that is repeated without further use of the drug that first caused it.

freebase   To purify cocaine under heat.

hallucinogen   Drug or chemical that causes hallucinations or distorted experiences.

impaired   Made worse.

60 | **inhibition** The act of holding back
certain behavior.

intoxication Loss of control of oneself
by use of alcohol or other drugs.

malnutrition Unhealthy condition of the
body caused by lack of proper food.

manslaughter The killing of a person
without previous intent to do so.

marijuana The dried leaves and flowers
of the hemp plant; a drug that is
smoked.

narcotic Drug such as morphine or
heroin that makes one feel dull and
may lessen pain.

nicotine Poisonous, oily liquid found in
tobacco leaves.

rehabilitation Process of bringing back
to a normal or good condition.

sedative Tending to calm.

solvent Substance that can dissolve
another.

stimulant Something that excites or
quickens, such as coffee or certain
drugs.

Help List

1-800-COCAINE
Cocaine Helpline
Monday through Friday
9:00 A.M.–3:00 A.M.
Saturday and Sunday
12:00 NOON–3:00 A.M.

1-800-544-KIDS
National Federation of
  Parents for Drug-Free
  Youth
Monday through Friday
9:00 A.M.–5:00 P.M.

1-800-662-HELP
National Institute on Drug
  Abuse
Information and Referral
  Line
Monday through Friday
8:30 A.M.–4:30 P.M.

1-800-662-2255
National Council on
  Alcoholism
7 days a week, 24 hours a day

1-800-9-FRIEND
Straight 24-Hour
Crisis Prevention
  Hotline

STOPP (Students To Offset
  Peer Pressure)
P.O. Box 103, Department S
Hudson, NH 03051-0103

SADD (Students Against
  Drunk Driving)
P.O. Box 800
Marlboro, MA 01752

Narcotics Anonymous
  World Service Office
16155 Wyandotte Street
Van Nuys, CA 91406

Telephone Book
Yellow Pages

Alcoholism, Drug Abuse,
Counselors

For Further Reading

Edwards, Gabrielle I. *Coping with Drug Abuse*. New York: Rosen Publishing Group, Inc. 1991.

Dupont, Robert. *Getting Tough on Gateway Drugs*. Washington, D.C.: American Psychiatric Press, 1984.

Gold, Mark S. *The Facts about Drugs and Alcohol*. New York: Lawrence Chilnick Associates, Inc., 1988.

Grosshandler, Janet. *Coping with Drinking and Driving*. New York: Rosen Publishing Group, Inc., 1990.

Hjelmeland, Andy. *Drinking and Driving*. New York: Crestwood House, Macmillan Publishing Company, 1990.

In Motion—The Student Guide to Safe Driving, "Peer Pressure—The Party's Over But the Painful Memory Lingers." Northbrook, IL: General Learning Corporation, 1990.

Newman, Susan. *You Can Say No to a Drink or Drug—What Every Kid Should Know*. New York: Putnam Publishing Group, Perigee Books, 1986.

Stearn, Marshall, B., Ph.D. *Drinking and Driving, Know Your Limits and Liabilities*. Sausalito, CA: Park West Publishing Co., 1985.

Index

About The Author

Janet Grosshandler is a guidance counselor at Jackson Memorial High School, Jackson, New Jersey.

She earned a B.A. at Trenton State College in New Jersey and followed soon after with an M.Ed. from Trenton while teaching seventh-grade English.

Coping with Verbal Abuse, Coping with Drinking and Driving, Coping with Alcohol Abuse, and *The Value of Generosity* are other books by Janet published by the Rosen Publishing Group, Inc.

Recently widowed, Janet lives in Jackson with her three young sons, Nate, Jeff, and Mike. She squeezes in time for running and reading.

Photo Credits
Cover: Stuart Rabinowitz
Photos on pages 2, 43, AP / Wide World Photos; all other photos by Stuart Rabinowitz

Design & Production: Blackbirch Graphics, Inc.

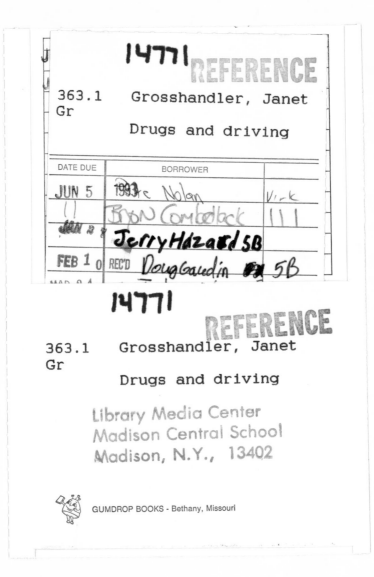

14771 REFERENCE

363.1
Gr

Grosshandler, Janet

Drugs and driving

DATE DUE	BORROWER	
JUN 5 1993	e Nolan	Virk
	Bron Combelack	111
JUN 2	JerryHazard 5B	
FEB 1 0 REC'D	DougGaudin 5B	

14771 REFERENCE

363.1
Gr

Grosshandler, Janet

Drugs and driving